Daniel Tucker

5 Ingredients Recipes for Slow Cooker:
Be Busy – Not Hungry!

D1563731

Table of Contents

Introduction

Have you ever found yourself trying to put together a nice meal for the whole family but were too busy or to cook everything from scratch? When you are a busy parent, worker or spread yourself too thin having to do many tasks at the same time, cooking can inevitably become a chore that you'll have to fulfill or else you and your family will starve--(unless, of course, you have the money to order from a takeaway).

Luckily, there are some cooking ways and tools that make the challenging and time-consuming task of cooking much easier and effortless. We don't know exactly who discovered the famous slow cooker/crockpot, but we owe them a huge favor as we can prepare meals in seconds and enjoy them a few hours later. Using a slow cooker to cook your next family meal, isn't as challenging as it appears to be and **the recipes you'll find on the present cookbook require only 5 ingredients and minimal tools to be prepared!**

Happy slow cooking!

Main Meal Recipes

Balsamic & Coriander Pork Roast

If you have a pork belly but don't want to go for the usual barbeque pork roast, try this Mediterranean/Cypriot style pork roast instead with coriander and balsamic vinegar for a more caramelised flavor.

Ingredients:

- Medium pork belly (around 10 pounds)
- 1 cup of balsamic vinegar
- 3 tbsp of crushed coriander
- 2 cloves of garlic
- Salt/Pepper

Directions:

- Season the pork belly with salt and pepper, massaging it over the skin to be penetrated.
- Cook with the rest of ingredients in low heat for 7 hours.

Bacon Mac & Cheese

A slow-cooker version of the famous, hearty bacon Mac & Cheese producing a really gooey and melt-in-your-mouth result that will be devoured for sure.

Ingredients:

- 2 cups of elbow pasta
- 5 thick slices of bacon, cut into small pieces
- 5 cups of milk
- 2 cups of mature cheddar cheese
- Garlic salt/pepper to taste

Directions:

- Lightly grease a shallow pan and saute the bacon for a couple of minutes until slightly brown on the edges.
- Add the pasta, milk, cheddar cheese, bacon and garlic salt and pepper to taste into the crockpot.

Set on high heat and cook for 4 hours.

Pizza-Pasta Bake

Since everyone loves pizza and pasta, you can combine the two in a single recipe like this one, featuring pepperoni and green peppers. Feel free to use other veggies e.g., olives or sweet corn or customize your cheeses.

Ingredients:

- 1 ½ cup of pasta
- 10-12 sliced of pepperoni
- 2 cups of tomato pasta sauce
- 2 green peppers sliced
- 2 cups of 4-cheese mix

Directions:

- Dilute the tomato sauce with 1 ½ cup of water and add to the slow cooker.
- Add the pasta. Follow with the peppers and the pepperoni slices.
- Bake everything in low heat for 4 hours.
- Sprinkle the cheese and bake for another 40 minutes on high heat.

Honey Mustard Pork Chops

These zesty, honey mustard pork chops combine ideally the famous honey-mustard mix for a simple yet perfect blend of sweet and sour and juicy pork chops that soft and cooked to perfection.

Ingredients (4 servings):

- 4-5 boneless pork chops
- 3 tbsp of mustard powder
- 1 tbsp of honey
- 2 cups of chicken stock
- 1 tsp of thyme

Directions:

- Mix in a bowl the mustard, honey, and chicken stock.
- Lightly oil the crockpot and add the pork chops.
- Pour the honey/mustard mixture over the pork chops.
- Set and cook on low heat for 4 ½ hours.

Onion Chicken & Stuffing

A traditional onion chicken recipe with a twist combining the flavors of chicken along with onion and stuffing for a nice winter or festive meal the whole family will enjoy.

Ingredients (4 servings):

- 4-5 chicken thighs (around 12 oz.)
- 1 large onion, sliced
- 1 sachet (around 3,5 oz.) of onion soup mix
- 1 pack of frozen chicken or turkey stuffing (around 10 oz.)
- 1 liter of chicken broth.

Directions:

- Lightly grease the crockpot surface and add the chicken thighs.
- Add the onions on top, the onion soup sachet and the chicken stuffing.
- Pour over the chicken broth, stir, and set on high heat for 4 hours.

Cauliflower Tomato and Chicken

A simple yet rich in flavor recipe made with cauliflower, tomato paste, and chicken lightly seasoned to enhance the flavors of the ingredients without being overpowering. The texture will closely resemble that of stew.

Ingredients:

- 2 cups of small cauliflower florets
- 3 whole boneless chicken thighs
- 1 ½ cup of pasta sauce diluted in a ½ cup of water
- 1 large onion, chopped
- Garlic salt

Directions:

- Combine all the ingredients in the slow cooker.
- Cook on low heat for 5 hours.

Basic Beef Stew with a Twist

A version of the famous Irish beef stew (beef slowly cooked with veggies and liquids) with the addition of Italian sausages for extra flavor.

Ingredients:

- 2 oz. of lean beef meat chunks
- 1 large onion chopped
- 2 medium carrots chopped
- 2 Italian sausages, sliced
- 1 ½ liter beef stock (with sodium)

Directions:

- Heat a bit of oil in a pan and saute the sliced sausages with the onions. Transfer to a bowl and set aside.
- Add the beef to the crockpot and pour over the beef stock. Set to low heat and cook for 4 hours.
- Add the chopped carrots, onions, and sausages onto to crockpot, lightly stir everything up and set to high heat for another 1½ hour.

Zesty Salmon & Asparagus

A healthy salmon recipe for fans of zesty flavors, paired with asparagus as an extra yet flavorful side dish. The recipe also requires less than 2 hours cooking time.

Ingredients:

- 3-4 skinned and deboned salmon fillets
- 1 cup of lemon juice (1 tsp of lemon zest also kept aside)
- 4-5 stalks of asparagus (peeled)
- Salt
- Lemon pepper

Directions:

- Add the salmon and asparagus into the crockpot, add the lemon juice and zest and season with salt and pepper
- Cook on low heat for 2 hours and serve.

Hearty Lentil Curry Soup

A simplified hearty lentil curry soup that is normally cooked in India, especially during the cold winter months with a mild spicy flavor, that isn't overwhelming.

Ingredients:

- 2 cups of dried black lentils
- 1 large onion, sliced
- 2 cloves of garlic, minced
- 3 tbsp. of curry powder
- 2 liters of vegetable broth (full sodium)

Directions:

- Saute in a small pan (lightly greased) the onions for a couple of minutes. Toss in the garlic and saute for another two minutes.
- Wash the dried lentils and add to the crockpot. Add the curry powder, onions, garlic and vegetable broth to the crockpot with the lentils. Stir.
- Set on low heat and cook overnight for 8 hours.

Healthy Asian Chicken & Veggies

If you are a fan of clean, Asian flavors and recipes, this recipe is perfect as it delicious and contains less than 180 calories per serving - chicken and veggies are the key ingredients of the recipe.

Ingredients (3-4 servings):

- 3 large chicken breasts
- 1 pack (around half an oz.) of mixed frozen veggies
- 2 cups of soy sauce
- 1 tbsp. of grated ginger
- 2 cups of low sodium vegetable broth

Directions:

- Combine in a medium bowl the soy sauce, ginger, and vegetable broth.
- Add the chicken and veggie mix to the crockpot.
- Pour over the soy sauce mixture and set to high heat for 4 hours.

Chilli Sausage Beef

The slow cooker version of the classic Chili beef paired with red beans for even more protein and flavor. Very easy to put together.

Ingredients:

- 2 oz. of ground beef (with a bit of fat)
- 2 sachets of chili seasoning mix
- 2 cups of dried red beans
- 1 ½ cup tomato sauce
- 1 liter of beef broth

Directions:

- Lightly oil a deep pan and saute the ground beef till it gets a light brown color. Season with salt and pepper.
- Add the ground beef to the crockpot and mix in the rest of the ingredients, giving everything a good stir.
- Set on high heat and cook for 3 ½ hours before serving alone.

Oriental/French Pulled Duck

A great pulled duck recipe inspired by Oriental and French restaurants that combines ideally the fatty taste and texture of the duck with the semi-sweet tanginess of orange juice and the sweetness of honey.

Ingredients:

- 1 medium whole duck, skinned (around 2 ½ pounds)
- 1 cup of orange juice
- 1 cup of soy sauce
- ½ cup of honey
- Salt/Pepper

Directions:

- Season the duck with salt and pepper from the inside out.
- Combine the liquids in a bowl.
- Place the duck in the slow cooker and pour over the soy sauce mixture.
- Cook in low heat for 7 hours.

Juicy Chicken Roast

The slow-cooker version of the famous and family favorite Sunday chicken roast with just the right amount of seasoning to make the chicken flavors popular.

Ingredients:

- 1 whole medium chicken, skinned
- 1 pack of mixed frozen veggies (around 1 oz.)
- 3 cloves of garlic, mashed
- 2 tbsp. of oregano or all purpose seasoning
- 2 cups of vegetable broth

Directions:

- Lightly oil the chicken and season with oregano or all purpose seasoning as well as salt inside and out.
- Add the chicken and add the veggies on the sides. Add the two cups of vegetable stock around the veggies and the chicken with the garlic cloves
- Set to low heat and cook for 8 hours.

Pulled Pork Barbeque & Beer

A great recipe for making pulled pork that is so tender that you can shred with a fork - the addition of ginger beer in this recipe adds a more tangy and rich flavor that blends nicely with pork.

Ingredients:

- 1 ⅕ lbs roast pork loin
- 2 cups of barbeque sauce
- 1 cup of ginger ale or beer
- 1 large onion, sliced
- Garlic Salt/Pepper

Directions:

- Season the pork loin with garlic salt and pepper.
- Add to the crockpot and arrange the onions on the side. Pour over the barbeque sauce and the ginger ale.
- Cook on low heat for 8 hours, shred the pork and serve ideally with a bun or coleslaw salad.

Black Bean & Tomato Chutney Soup

If you are a fan of black beans, try this easy, hearty soup made with black beans and tomato chutney instead of tomato sauce, which adds a more mild and interesting taste compared to regular tomato sauce.

Ingredients:

- 1 cup of dried black beans
- 1 large onion, chopped
- ⅓ cup tomato chutney
- ⅓ cup corn
- 1 liter of chicken broth

Directions:

- Saute the onion first in a lightly oil pan and combine with the rest of ingredients in the crockpot.
- Cook on low heat for 6 hours.

Marsala Wine Beef

This recipe below calls for the use of Marsala wine, which is very aromatic, semi-sweet Italian wine variety producing a rich caramelized flavor which pairs rather nicely with beef. The result will be an extra rick and tender beef.

Ingredients:

- 3 pounds of boneless beef chuck
- 3 scallions cut in half
- 1 1/2 cup of marsala red wine
- 1 tbsp. of butter
- Salt/Pepper to taste

Directions:

- Combine all the ingredients in the slow cooker.
- Cook in low heat for 7 hours.

Teriyaki Chicken Wings

Chicken Teriyaki is a famous Japanese dish with teriyaki soy sauce that you can also prepare in your slow cooker. This recipe calls for chicken wings that are more kid and family-friendly but you can use whole chicken thighs or pieces if you like.

Ingredients:

- 8-10 chicken wings (joints removed)
- 1 cup of Teriyaki sauce
- 1 tbsp. of ginger paste
- 1 tbsp. of honey
- 1 tsp of red chilli flakes

Directions:

- Combine all the seasonings with the teriyaki sauce and honey in a bowl and stir well.
- Shallow fry the chicken wings on a grill pan with a tiny amount of oil in high heat till the change color.
- Transfer to the slow cooker with the teriyaki mix and bake on high heat for 3 hours.

Fragrant Meatballs & Tomato

Fancy some Italian inspired meatballs? Try this recipe for fully juicy and tender meatballs with the addition of bacon for a touch of smoky flavor and serve them with pasta or as they are - your children will love it.

Ingredients:

- 1 pound of ground beef and pork (half of each)
- ½ cup of chopped parsley
- 2 tbsp. of Italian seasoning
- 5 slices of bacon, cut into pieces
- 2 cups of tomato sauce diluted in one cup of water

Directions:

- In a bowl, combine together the ground meats, parsley, Italian seasoning, salt, and pepper.
- Saute the bacon bits in a small frying pan until light brown on the edges. Add to the meatball mixture and shape into small balls.
- Add the tomato sauce and water into the crockpot. Place the meatballs over the sauce.
- Cook on low heat for 6 hours prior serving.

Easy Lasagna Beef Noodles

A great gooey lasagna recipe with beef and tomato filling that's perfect for lunch or dinner. Can also be made in batches and put in the freezer afterward.

Ingredients:

- 1 pound of ground beef
- 3 cups of tomato pasta sauce
- 1 tbsp. of Italian seasoning
- 1 pack of lasagna sheets (around 5-6 lasagna sheets)
- 2 cups of grated parmesan or cheddar sauce

Directions:

- Lightly grease a frying pan and saute the ground beef. Cook for a couple of minutes until brown and add 1 cup of the pasta sauce. Season with Italian seasoning and salt to taste.
- Arrange one layer of lasagna into the crockpot. Add a thick layer of the beef mixture with a spoon, sprinkle some cheese and repeat the same process until you use the last lasagna sheet.
- Add the remaining pasta sauce and sprinkle with the rest of the cheese.
- Cook on high heat for 4 hours

Steak & Jacket Potatoes

Steak and jacket potatoes are a favorite combo of the British and this recipe is a simple yet fully flavored version of the classic steak and potatoes prepared separately in the oven or stovetop.

Ingredients:

- 1 1.5 lb. of round beef steak
- 4 big potatoes, washed (with the peel on)
- One onion thinly sliced
- Peppercorn
- Garlic Salt

Directions:

- Wrap the potatoes in aluminum foil and place first on the slow cooker.
- In a flat board, season the steak with peppercorn and garlic salt (add a splash of olive oil optional).
- Add the stake on top of the potatoes and cook in high heat for 5 hours.
- Take off the potatoes and add onions on top. Cook for another hour in low heat.
- Serve the steak with the jacket potatoes filled with melted butter and chives.

Greek Ouzo Chicken

Ouzo is a Greek alcoholic spirit made of anise extract that has a mildly sweet flavor and is often accompanies meat and seafood. Try this unique recipe for a fragrant moist chicken that will surely impress your guests.

Ingredients:

- One chicken, cut into skinless bone-in pieces (around 3 lbs)
- 1 cup of Greek ouzo
- 1 tbsp of oregano or greek seasoning
- 3 tbsp of olive oil
- Salt/Pepper

Directions:

- Smother the chicken pieces in the olive oil and rub them with the greek seasoning, salt, and pepper.
- Add these to the crockpot and pour over them ouzo.
- Cook in low heat for 7 hours.

Juicy Coca-Cola Spare Ribs

A finger-licking recipe of pork spare ribs combining the usual barbeque sauce with a bit of coca cola for a richer, more caramelized flavor. The result will be extra juicy and tender spare ribs that fall off the bone.

Ingredients:

- 3 lbs. of pork spare ribs
- 2 cups of barbeque sauce.
- 1 can of coca cola
- 2 tbsp. of oil
- 2 tbsp. of garlic salt

Directions:

- Smother the ribs with one cup of barbeque sauce and garlic salt and let marinade for at least 1 hour in the fridge.
- Place the ribs into the slow cooker; pour over the coca cola and the oil.
- Let cook on low heat for 7 hours.

Chickpeas Biryani Simplified

Biryani is a famous Indian recipe with tomato, curry, garam masala, and chicken/goat as its base together with other spices. This recipe is simplified vegan version of the classic Biryani with just 5 ingredients.

Ingredients:

- 2 cups of dried chickpeas
- 2 cups of tomato pasta sauce diluted in 2 cups of water
- 1 large onion, cut into big chunks
- 3 tbsp. of curry powder
- 1 tbsp. of grated ginger

Directions:

- Combine all the ingredients and add to the slow cooker.
- Cook on high heat for 5 hours.

Creamy Chicken Soup

There is nothing more comforting than a creamy chicken soup and veggies during cold winter nights (or days). Make this ahead for a hearty recipe loved by everyone.

Ingredients:

- 1 medium whole chicken (around 2 1/2 lbs.)
- 2 cans of cream of chicken soup
- 2 carrots, thickly sliced
- 2 celery stalks, sliced
- 1 liter of low sodium chicken broth

Directions:

- Combine everything together in the slow cooker.
- Stir and let cook for 6 hours on low heat.

Fish Fajitas

Although the use of meat is the norm when it comes to Mexican fajitas, you can also use fish to create tender and vegetarian fajitas if you love fish - the spices and peppers make plain boring fish taste extra tasty here in this recipe.

Ingredients:

- 3 tilapia fish fillets
- 1 green pepper, sliced
- 1 large red onion, sliced
- 3 tbsp. of Fajita Seasoning
- 1 cup of tomato juice

Directions:

- Rub the tilapia fish fillets in fajita seasoning and lightly season with salt.
- Add the fish fillets with the rest of ingredients.
- Cook on high heat for 2 hours.
- Serve on tortillas with guacamole, sour cream, and Pico de Gallo.

Veggie Pork Meatloaf

A moist and flavorful meatloaf recipe with pork and veggies for extra flavor and nutritional value. If you are fed up with the ordinary beef meatloaf with livery texture, you will love this.

Ingredients:

- 1 pound of ground pork
- Half a pack of mixed frozen veggies (around 10 oz.)
- 1 tbsp. of soy sauce
- 1 tbsp. of garlic salt
- ½ cup of tomato ketchup

Directions:

- In a shallow frying pan combine the veggies and season with garlic salt. Finish off with the soy sauce.
- Add the veggies and sauce to the ground pork and half of the ketchup, combine well, and transfer the mixture into a 9X5 in. loaf pan.
- Bake in high heat for 3 ½ hours. Add the rest of the tomato ketchup on top and bake for another hour on high heat.

Vodka & Dill Salmon

If you have some fresh or frozen salmon fillets, this simple yet full of flavor recipe balances nicely the rich fatty taste and texture of salmon with a vodka and lime for extra tanginess. Try it!

Ingredients:

- 4 boneless and skinless salmon fillets
- 1 tbsp of dill
- ½ cup of vodka
- ½ cup of lime juice
- Garlic salt

Directions:

- Season the salmon fillets with the dill and garlic salt and add to the slow cooker.
- Pour the vodka and lime juice.
- Cook on high heat for 2 hours.

Pork Belly in Wine

This braised pork belly slowly cooked with wine is perfect for all occasions - from family dinners to parties and the addition of smoked paprika adds a touch of smoky flavor to this rich and juicy dish.

Ingredients:

- 1 ½ pounds pork belly
- 1 tbsp. of smoked paprika
- 2 tbsp. of garlic salt
- 2 cups of red wine
- 1 cup of beef broth

Directions:

- Season the pork belly with the smoked paprika and garlic salt and let sit on the fridge for at least two hours.
- Transfer the belly to the slow cooker, pour the red wine and beef broth on top.
- Bake for 7 hours on low heat.

Candied Sweet Potatoes

Candied Sweet Potatoes with brown sugar are very common in festive meals like Christmas and Thanksgiving and you can prepare this side dish to accompany your turkey/chicken and stuffing using your slow cooker. Here is the recipe:

Ingredients:

- 3 large sweet potatoes, peeled and sliced thickly
- 1 cup of brown sugar
- 1 cup of melted butter or margarine
- 1 tbsp. of cinnamon
- ½ cup of water

Directions:

- Arrange the potatoes, and add the rest of the ingredients on top, lightly stirring everything together.
- Bake on low heat for 5 hours.

Mexican Pork Carnitas

Mexican Pork Carnitas are basically a version of pulled or at least tender pork pieces seasoned with Mexican spices and paired with peppers and onions. You can prepare extra juicy and tender carnitas using this recipe.

Ingredients:

- 4 pounds pork butt or shoulder
- 2 red peppers chopped
- 1 large onion chopped
- 2 tbsp. of Mexican or taco seasoning
- 1 cup of lime juice

Directions:

- Season the pork shoulder with taco seasoning and salt/pepper.
- Lightly oil your slow cooker and add the veggies and the pork shoulder together with the lime juice.
- Cook for 8 hours on low heat.

Oxtails & Rice

Oxtails are one of the cheapest beef cuts and you can make a heart oxtail rice soup that will keep you satisfying. The wine here in this recipe adds a touch of sour and fragrant note.

Ingredients:

- 3 pounds of oxtail, thickly cut
- 1 large onion, chopped
- 1 liter of beef broth
- 2 cups of basmati rice
- ½ dry white wine

Directions:

- Lightly grease the crockpot surface and add everything together, stirring lightly to combine.
- Cook in low heat for 5 hours.

Tomato and Pea Orzo Soup

A hearty soup with orzo in its base, tomato, and peas that is 100% vegan and requires absolutely no preparation whatsoever to be cooked other than adding all the ingredients in the slow cooker.

Ingredients:

- 1 1/2pack of orzo pasta
- 1 cup of tomato
- ½ cup of frozen peas
- 1 ½ liter of chicken broth
- A splash of olive oil

Directions:

- Combine all the ingredients together in the crockpot.
- Cook on high heat for 3 ½ hours.

Chicken & Mushroom Risotto

If you are a fan of rich, creamy, and earthy tastes, you will love this chicken risotto recipe which is paired with mushrooms and cream of mushroom soup for a burst of meaty-like flavor minus the meat.

Ingredients:

- 2 chicken thighs, cut into thick pieces
- ½ of chopped white mushrooms
- 1 can of mushroom soup
- 1 ½ cup rice
- 1 liter of water.

Directions:

- Lightly grease a pan and saute the mushrooms (season with salt and pepper).
- Combine the mushrooms with the rice and the rest of the ingredients to the crockpot
- Cook in low heat for 5 hours.

Easy Seafood Paella

Paella is a popular Spanish dish made or rice and seafood with minimal seasoning and use of veggies to avoid covering the fresh seafood flavors

Ingredients:

- 2 cups of long grain rice
- 1 small pack (around 10 oz.) of mixed seafood
- 1 tbsp of saffron
- 1 scallion, roughly chopped
- 3 cups of chicken broth

Directions:

- Combine all the ingredients together in the slow cooker.
- Cook for 2 ½ hours on high heat.

Thai Chilli Chicken

Thai Chilli Chicken is chicken smothered in a spicy, sour, and sweet red chilli sauce. Try this simple Thai Chilli recipe for a more tender version of the dish.

Ingredients:

- 3 large chicken breasts (around 1 ½ lbs.)
- 1 cup of red chilli sauce diluted in a ½ cup of water
- 1 tbsp. of sesame oil
- 2 spring onions, sliced
- Garlic salt

Directions:

- Season the chicken breasts with the garlic salt.
- Add the chicken breast with the rest of ingredients to the slow cooker.
- Cook in low heat for 6 hours.

Spicy Black-Eyed Bean Soup

If you like black-eyed peas but looking for new ways to incorporate them into your kitchen meals or if you are vegan, this black-eyed soup is perfect and the addition of spice also adds extra flavor and heat.

Ingredients:

- 1 ½ cup of dried black-eyed beans
- 1 large onion, chopped
- 1 cup of pasta sauce
- 1 liter of veggie broth
- 1 tbsp. of chilli flakes

Directions:

- Combine all the ingredients in the crockpot.
- Bake on low heat for 7 hours.

Lemon & Caper Pork Chops

Forget boring tasting, rubbery, or too saucy pork chops. This recipe here is zesty and flavorsome without being too dry or saucy. Serve this with plain rice and salad for a fully complete meal.

Ingredients:

- 4 thickly cut pork chops
- 1 cup of lemon juice
- 2 tbsp. of capers
- 1 cup of chicken broth
- Salt/Pepper

Directions:

- Lightly oil the pork chops and combine with the rest of the ingredients in the slow cooker.
- Bake on high heat for 4 hours.

Sweet and Sour Gammon

Pork/Ham legs and tenderloins are perfect for the slow cooker, as they need more than 3 hours of cooking to be prepared traditionally. This recipe is a sweet and sour version of gammon, which is perfect for festive meals for your family or guests.

Ingredients:

- 1 cured ham leg/gammon (around 8 pounds)
- 1 cup of sweet and sour sauce
- 1 can of chopped pineapples or freshly chopped pineapple slices
- 1 cup of low sodium veggie broth
- Salt/Pepper

Directions:

- Place the ham into the crockpot with the rest of ingredients
- Bake on low heat for 7 hours.

Roast Lamb Leg

If you love lamb, this recipe is ideal for producing a tender juicy lamb leg with the mild flavors and scents of mint and rosemary, which give this lamb leg another dimension.

Ingredients:

- 1 boneless leg of lamb nested (around 7 pounds)
- 20 cloves of garlic
- 3 tbsp. of mint
- 2 fresh rosemary sprigs
- Salt/Pepper

Directions:

- Make small incisions with a knife (around twenty) throughout the lamp leg and insert the garlic cloves.
- Take the nest away, season with mint and salt/pepper and add to the crockpot with the rosemary on the sides.
- Cook for 8 hours on low heat.

Glazed Salmon

An Asian-inspired glazen salmon dish made with salmon fillets and soy sauce along with honey for extra sweetness and ginger paired with chilli flakes for extra heat.

Ingredients:

- 4-5 skinless salmon fillets
- 1 cup of soy sauce
- ½ cup of maple syrup
- 1 tbsp of ginger paste
- 1 tsp of red chilli flakes

Directions:

- Combine all the ingredients except from the salmon in a bowl and stir well.
- Add the salmon fillets to the slow cooker and pour the sauce on top.
- Cook on high heat for 2 hours.

Pumpkin & Ginger Soup

Pumpkin is the protagonist of fall and winter recipes and if you fancy some twist to the ordinary pumpkin soup recipe, try this recipe with ginger.

Ingredients:

- 1 small pumpkin (around 1 oz.), cut into pieces
- 1 tbsp of ginger paste
- 1 medium, potato, peeled and roughly chopped
- 1 1/2 liter of full sodium vegetable broth
- 1 tbsp of cinnamon

Directions:

- Combine all the ingredients in the slow cooker.
- Cook in low heat for five hours.
- Blend to form a thick veloute soup.

Bean & Sausage Risotto

Beans and Sausage go perfectly together and you'll realize this in this rich, creamy bean and sausage risotto slowly cooked to perfection.

Ingredients:

- 1 cup of risotto rice, washed and drained
- 1 cup of white beans
- 2 Italian sausages, roughly chopped
- 1 liter of beef broth
- 1 tbsp of parmesan cheese

Directions:

- Combine everything together except the parmesan.
- Stir and cook on high heat for 3 hours.
- Add the parmesan cheese.
- Cook for half an hour on high heat.

Stuffed Turkey Breasts

Love some turkey but don't want to use/cook a whole turkey for convenience reasons? Try this stuffed turkey breast recipe with ham and cheese. It almost tastes like chicken but it's even juicier and more flavorful.

Ingredients:

- 3 large turkey breasts, tenderized
- 4 picnic ham slices
- 3 slices of American cheese
- 1 cup of tomato sauce
- 1 tbsp of garlic salt

Directions:

- Add one slice of ham and one slice of cheese onto each chicken breast and roll from one side to another securing with a toothpick.
- Place the stuffed turkey breasts into the slow cooker, pour the tomato sauce on top and the garlic salt.
- Cook in low heat for 5 hours.

Chicken Noodle Soup

There is nothing more comforting for the whole family than a chicken and noodle soup. It's so healthy yet so flavorful and you only need onions and tomatoes as your veggies to make this recipe.

Ingredients:

- 1 medium chicken, skinless, in pieces (bone-in)
- 1 ½ liter of vegetable broth
- 1 cup of minestrone pasta (or any other small pasta)
- 2 fresh onions, chopped
- ½ cup of tomato paste

Directions:

- Combine everything together in the slow cooker.
- Cook for 6 hours on low heat.

Easy Seafood Chowder

Chowder is a popular U.S hybrid of a creamy thick soup and a stew, typically using seafood, fish and veggies with creamy ingredients. As the basic recipe calls for more than 8 ingredients, we have made this simpler without sacrificing flavor.

Ingredients:

- ½ cup shellfish
- 1 cup of vegetable or coconut cream
- 2 scallions, sliced
- 3 bacon slices, thinly cut
- 1 liter of fish stock

Directions:

- Saute the onions with the bacon in a pan.
- Combine with the rest of the ingredients in the slow cooker.
- Cook in low heat for 3 hours.

Orzo & Peppers risotto

A Mediterranean inspired recipe that calls for the use of orzo instead of rice for a more rich texture and flavor together with peppers and tomato sauce as the main ingredients.

Ingredients:

- 3 large green peppers, chopped
- 1 cup of orzo
- 2 scallions, chopped
- 1 cup of tomato sauce
- 2 ½ cups of vegetable broth

Directions:

- Saute the scallions with the peppers in a bit of olive oil for 1-2 minutes.
- Combine with the remaining ingredients in the slow cooker.
- Cook in low heat for 4 hours.

Easy Ratatouille

Ratatouille is a popular French dish made of cubed veggies with different variations across southern Europe. Here is a very simple version of the dish that is still fully delicious.

Ingredients:

- 2 large zucchini, cubed
- 2 eggplants, cubed
- One large onion, chopped
- 1 cup of tomato sauce
- ½ liter of vegetable broth

Directions:

- Saute the onions, eggplants, and zucchini in a greased pan for only 2 minutes
- Combine with the rest of ingredients.
- Cook for 2 ½ hours in high heat.

Tuna & Pea 'Casserole'

This recipe is for making a unique Casserole combo with tuna and frozen peas, which is perfect for breakfast, lunch, or dinner and almost any season. This will quickly become a family favorite.

Ingredients:

- 2 fresh tuna fillets (boneless), cut into medium thick pieces
- 1 cup of frozen peas
- 1 can of cream of onion soup diluted in 1 cup of water
- 1 tsp of orange zest
- 1 cup of croutons

Directions:

- Combine all the ingredients together except the croutons and cook on low heat for 3 hours.
- Add the croutons.
- Cook for an extra hour in high heat.

Turkish Lamb Stew 'Tas Kebap'

Lamb is a staple in Muslim countries and "Tas Kebap" was a Turkish/Greek recipe that was cooked frequently in Smyrna homes. Try this simplified version for a no-fuss yet delicious result.

Ingredients:

- 1 pound of beef cubes (ideally chuck)
- 3 cloves of garlic
- 2 cups of tomato sauce
- 1 tbsp of cumin
- 1 tsp of cinnamon

Directions:

- Combine all the ingredients into the slow cooker.
- Cook on low heat for 7-8 hours.

Cajun Turkey Breasts

If you are a fan of Southern Cajun flavors, try this moist turkey breast cajun spice recipe instead of ordinary chicken or meat and you will be impressed on how simple yet flavorful this is.

Ingredients:

- 3 large turkey breasts
- 2 tbsp of cajun seasoning mix
- ½ cup of lime juice
- 1 tbsp of oil
- Garlic Salt

Directions:

- Lightly oil the turkey breasts and season with the Cajun seasoning mix and the garlic salt.
- Place the turkey breasts into the slow cooker.
- Cook in low heat for 5 hours.

5 Dessert Bonuses

Zesty Peach Cobbler

Making the popular peach cobbler couldn't be easier with your slow cooker - the peaches are nicely caramelized and the quick Bisquick mix used on top adds the necessary crunch with no fuss.

Ingredients:

- 4 cups of fresh or frozen skinned peach halves
- ⅓ cup brown sugar
- 1 tsp of cinnamon
- 1 tsp of orange zest
- 2 cups of Bisquick mix

Directions:

- Combine all the ingredients except the Bisquick mix in bowl to mix well and place them into the slow cooker, in low heat for 4 hours.
- Add the Bisquick mix diluted in a ⅔ cup of milk and cook for another hour in high heat.

Stevia Forest Berry Jam

Since forest fruits are available fresh or frozen, you can take advantage of their sweet tangy flavor with this healthier berry jam slow cooker version, sweetened with stevia.

Ingredients:

- 1 pack (around half a pound) mixed berries/strawberries, thawed and drained.
- ⅔ cup of stevia
- 1 tbsp of lemon juice
- 1 tsp vanilla extract
- 1 tsp of nutmeg

Directions:

- Combine and stir all the ingredients together in the slow cooker.
- Cook on low heat for 4 hours.

Caramelized Apples & Cinnamon

Apples and Cinnamon go nicely together and make perfect fall desserts. If you like them but want to try a more caramelized and sweet version of the combo, here is the recipe to follow.

Ingredients:

- 4 medium tart baking apples peeled.
- 3 tbsp of sugar
- ⅓ cup melted butter
- ½ tsp of ground cinnamon
- 1 tsp of vanilla extract

Directions:

- Combine the butter and sugar with the vanilla extract
- Place the apples in a lightly greased crockpot and sprinkle with the sugar mixture.
- Cook on low heat for 2 ½ hours.

Pumpkin Spice Cake

Have some leftover pumpkin - try this moist and flavorful pumpkin spice cake that is so easy that even a kid can make it. Goes nicely with coffee or a cup of tea.

Ingredients:

- 1 box (around 15.2 oz) spice cake mix
- ⅓ cup of pumpkin puree
- 3 eggs beaten with a ½ cup of milk
- 1 tsp of cinnamon
- 1 tsp of vanilla extract

Directions:

- Beat together all the ingredients and transfer the mixture into a heavily greased slow cooker surface.
- Cook on high heat for 1 hour and 40 minutes.

Chocolate Chip Scones

A unique recipe combining the soft, airy texture of scones with semi-sweet chocolate chip cookies that your family and kids especially will love. It's very easy and you can get your kids involved in it as well.

Ingredients:

- 1 cup of self-raising flour
- ⅓ cup of unsalted butter, melted
- 2 full tsp of light brown sugar
- ⅔ cups of milk
- ½ of semi-sweet chocolate chip cookies (frozen)

Directions:

- Combine the sugar with the flour.
- Add the butter, stir, and add the milk to make a fluffy soft dough. Knead with your hands or mixer.
- Add the chocolate chip cookies to the dough, slowly incorporating with your hands and transfer into the greased crockpot surface.
- Bake for 80 minutes on high heat.

Conclusion

The purpose of the present book was to give you 50+ ideas on preparing delicious meals for the whole family easily with minimal preparation and you'll realize if you try these recipes that you only need 5 ingredients and nothing more to make something nice.

When using your slow cooker, it is important to keep in mind a few basics so you don't end up with any disasters and mushy/ruined food. The first rule depends on the type of food you will use--meats, in general, require more hours to be fully baked, especially if they have bones or exceed 3 lbs in weight. For best results, cook meats in low heat for 5-8 hours. Veggies on the other hand and fish require much less time to be fully cooked and are best cooked in high heat for no more than 3 hours. In addition, some foods and ingredients do not tend to cook well in the slow cooker and these are chicken skins, seafood, milk/heavy cream and turkey bacon. Lean cuts of meat that do not contain any fat and are tender on their own e.g. pork tenderloin, may get hard and overcooked in the slow cooker.

As many recipes call for the use of frozen veggies, it would be better to thaw and drain them first and they will release excess moisture when slowly cooked and ruin the texture of the recipe into a runny, mushy mess.

While we have tried our best to include recipes that don't disintegrate or become a creamy/ruined mess, because slow cookers have varying temperatures, it would be wise to check your slow cooker every hour or so to see the progress of the food and cook it more or less as you see fit.

Also, keep in mind that the above recipes are designed to yield 4 servings on average so feel free to adjust the measures if you have a family of more or less than 4 people.

Extra tips:
- You can do some meal prep and prepare a few slow cooker meals in advance, store in an airtight Ziploc bag, and keep in the freezer until you are able to use them. Some recipes from the book are perfect for the freezer but make sure they don't contain many liquids and sauces other than the basic seasoning or juices or they will become a runny mess when baked on the slow cooker.
- Avoid over-stuffing your slow cooker. Doing so will increase its total cooking time and some of the juice and liquids may come on top. The above recipes work for most crockpot/slow cooker capacities but if your slow cooker has a capacity of less than 4 quarts, you may need to adjust the amount of ingredients so that you ideally cover no more than $\frac{2}{3}$ of your slow cooker.

Good luck and happy slow cooking.

Made in the USA
Lexington, KY
08 April 2019